where is identity and how do i get there

koshi

ARCHWAY
PUBLISHING

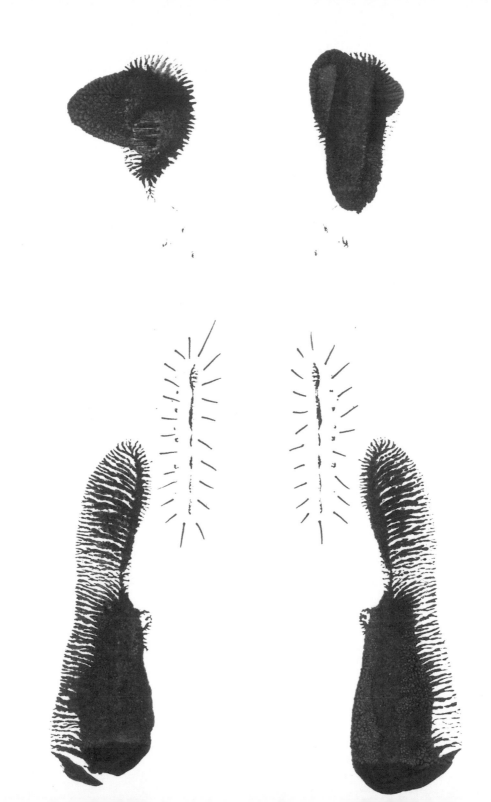

there's a dent in i-dent-ity

words are perfect as they are
it's our thoughts that give them flaws

giraffe and llama missing some body parts

¿cómo se llama?

in courage there's a rage
yes that crazy anger
that nobody wants to hear you talk about
it comes from the pain of knowing
you have no choice but to over-come

come can be a great relief

i dey come go
a local oxymoronic expression
its variant is i dey go come

i don't care what gender
you subscribe to
everyone needs a pair
even if it's a nonpair
ask nana

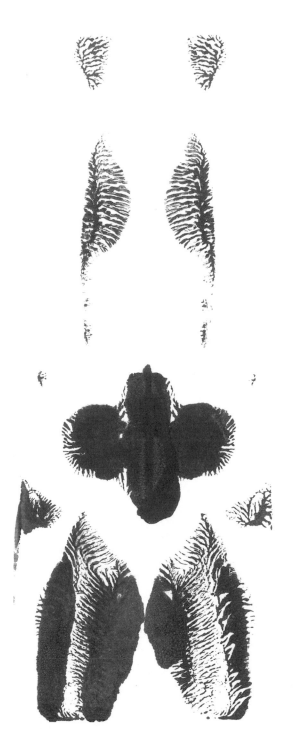

lilah would tell you
beautiful eye-lashes

fine pair right there

if i say so

lost pair

duplicating malariart parasites

symptoms of malariart

cyclical fevers in the brain
chills and cracks in the membrane
episodes of strange and vibrant vomitting
verbal diarrhea

doctor is my condition fatal

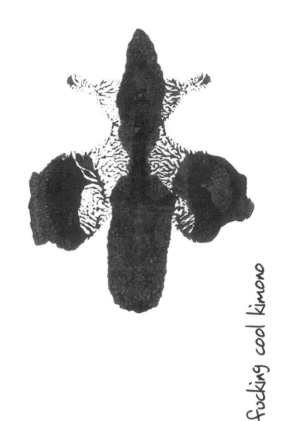

fucking cool kimono

do you drool
when you sleep
i already know you fart
f-art
don't you just love this word
very irreverently artsy
no wonder kids adore it

synchronicity is a
cosmic stopwatch

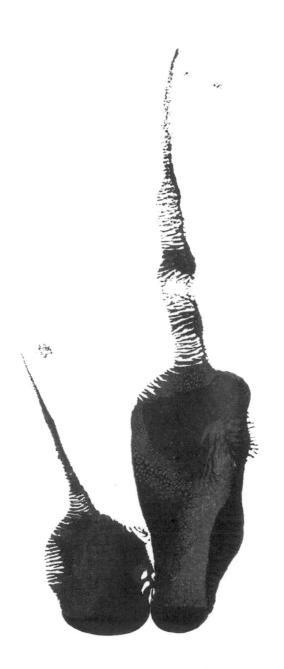

dear carl
i will always miss you
thank you for your earthly visit
it's still having an impact
i'm sorry you felt like you had
misplaced your soul but just so you know
your search was not in vain as it's
helping others find theirs

in the course

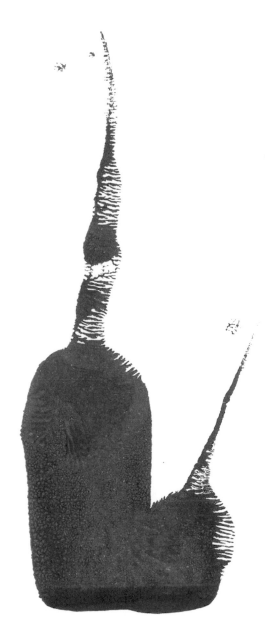

your central nervous system isn't a
reality snob
whether it's an incident a dream or
a spell of active imagination
CNS (pronounced sense) registers them all
as real and files them in your memory banks
under lived experience
to be retrieved as needed
what a fucking genius

of a coollision

one of my favorite works by dalí is
darkness and light a brilliant depiction of
self image

a wise child standing in front
of an ancient boulder

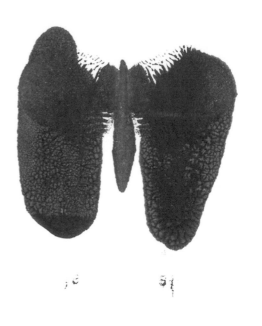

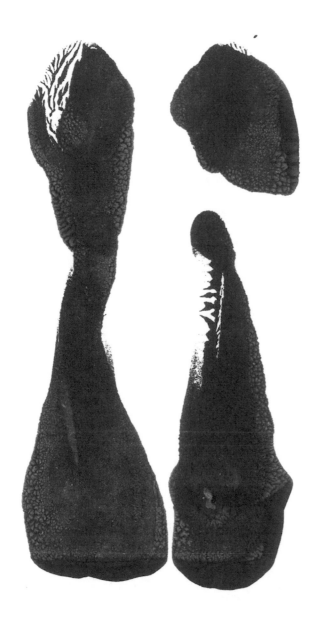

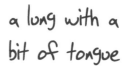

a lung with a
bit of tongue

it takes a creative tribe
to raise an adult
and barring that
almost any child will do

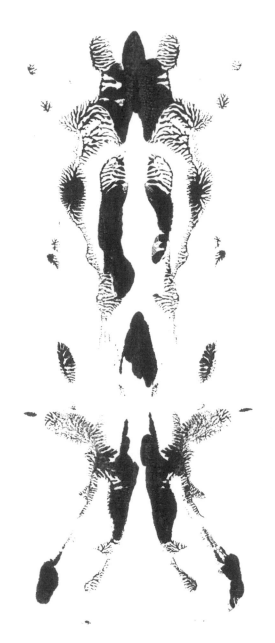

in arabic wa means and
and hala means welcome
in pidgin wahalla can be
a little bit of trouble
small wahalla
or a whole shitload of it
big wahalla
what if we were to celebrate
happy wahalla day

what interesting words do you
carry in your identity basket

oh pɨdɔiɑ
the french are quite serious
about their prostitutes

small wahalla that ends well

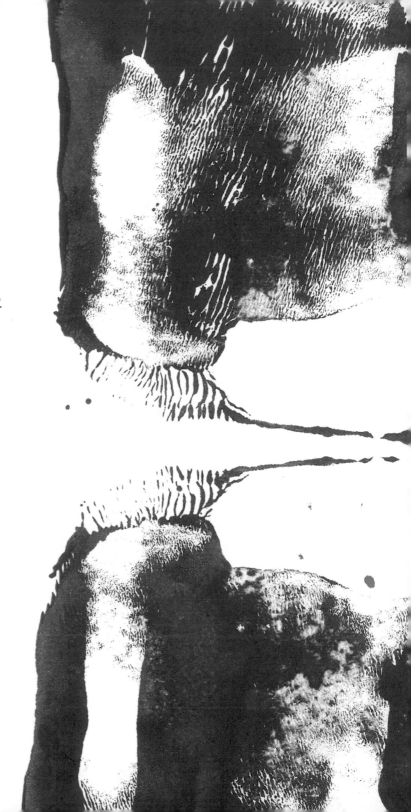

awake in sleep

your light is my shadow

traveler to the unknown

alone

in the dark i see

the many faces of your silence

an open mind

with broken corners

together we rise

my chains are your freedom

at home

the two great gifts
that seldom get any
likes
solitude and the
gift of not knowing

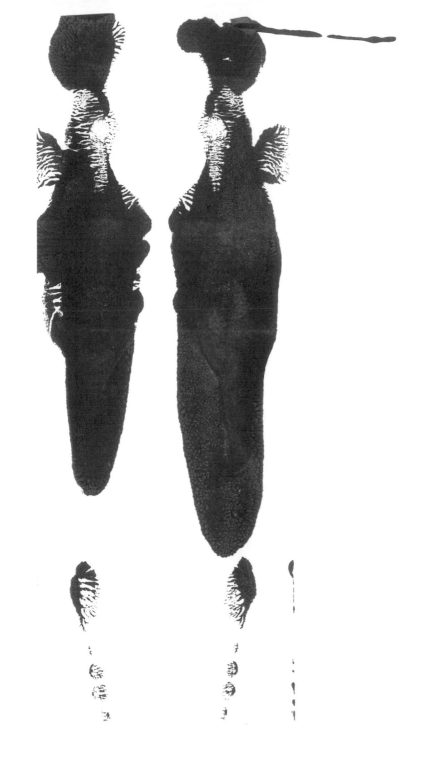

mirror mirror
in the skull
who's the sanest
of them all

is wellbeing on your bucket list
would you like to live there

left page
self denial with droopy boobies

not so right page
lady birds of a feather

to con-form
is to trick yourself or others
into believing
you
fit

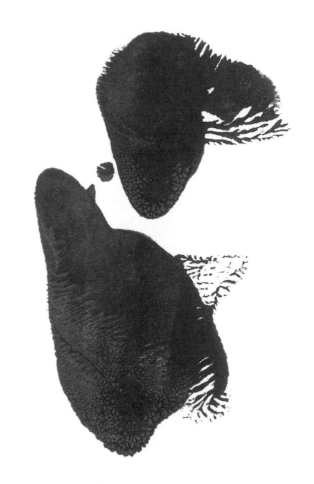

when social media was born
the social became terminally ill

are you allowing your thoughts
to hijack your feelings
thoughts don't have free will
you do

teenagers off-loading

the only thing
cancel culture seems
to be good at is
canceling our brain cells

media
for something that's
supposed to mediate
there's quite a bit of
dividing going on

if to listen is an art
and to speak is an art
what is good conversation
is there such a thing as an art times two
or two times an art

pregnant bitch
puppies are coming
there are six of them
get the fuck outta my way

lesley is one of the best conversationalists i know

portrait of an issue

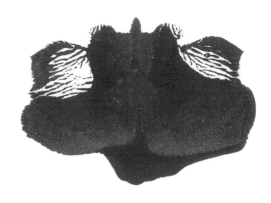

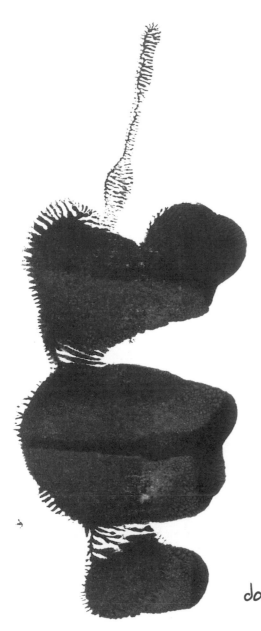

dog-ma is a dog with big issues
you're probably thinking
how can a dog have issues
well see it's about the issues themselves
they don't discriminate

dog with a fork in the eye

beauty on the rise

common wisdom says
beauty is in the eye of the beholder
well first of all it sounds painful
who wants to have anything
no matter how beautiful
>in< the eye
and secondly you gotta ask yourself
which one of them
and this applies to both the eye and the beholder
if you look closely enough at yourself
you may yet find many eyes
and many possible beholders

can you ever belong to someone
can they belong to you
i'm yours
you're mine
goose bumps and heart flutters
just saying
the only things we ever own
are those we've purchased

heck not even your kids belong to you
and though they may own most of your attention
but it's ok you can keep your toothpaste

starry night in accra

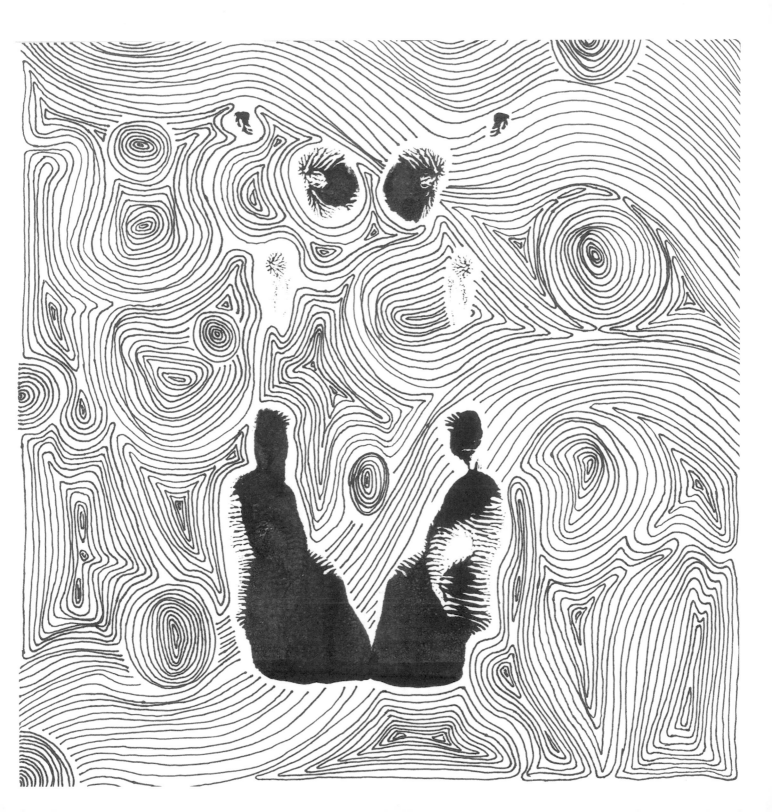

sex is what everybody's doing
above a certain age of course
and if they're not
they wanna be doing it
on second thought
luisa says her flatmate's really not into it
like bleah
hear that sigmund
you're screwed

deep play is the art
of dancing outside yourself
it is also how children
learn and achieve great growth
do you think you have nothing left
to learn
is that why you've stopped playing
too old too fat
too busy too important
too sad

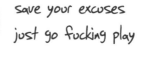

save your excuses
just go fucking play

soft play is fun with no strings attached
deep play is how you find yourself

don't you just love a well turned out head wrap

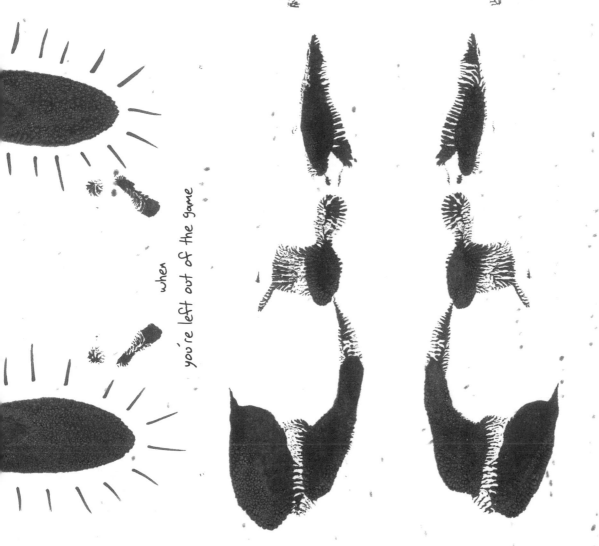

when
you're left out of the game

who doesn't like to play

identity like information is
a collective noun

freedom
also pronounced free-damnnn

- the madness to practice what-if
- the courage to fall flat on your face
- the strength to shovel your own shit
- the joy of not giving a damn

firebird flying into six suns

fiery dust

who do you care for
who cares for you
if you think of love as
con-flict
pay attention to the word
it starts with a lie

the grander your house is
the less likely it's going to be your home

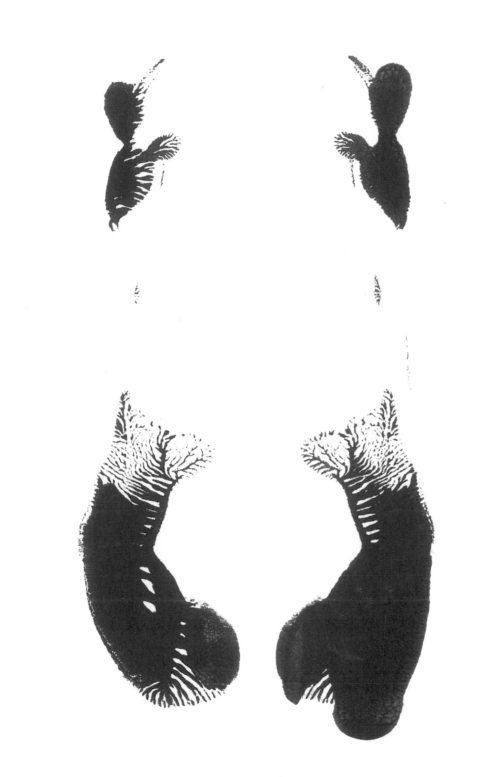

fancy hourglass
hour is the same as our
with a silent
exhale

everyday is
kiss-mas

ehein is one of these iconic words
with great charisma and staying power
not to mention versatility
it can be short
a simple question mark
or an invitation to go on
it can be a musical filler
or a sharp that's it got it
a shared moment over
a meeting of minds
when it's elongated
it means business
who the fuck are you messing with
i'll show you sense
and when you're done
it means the end

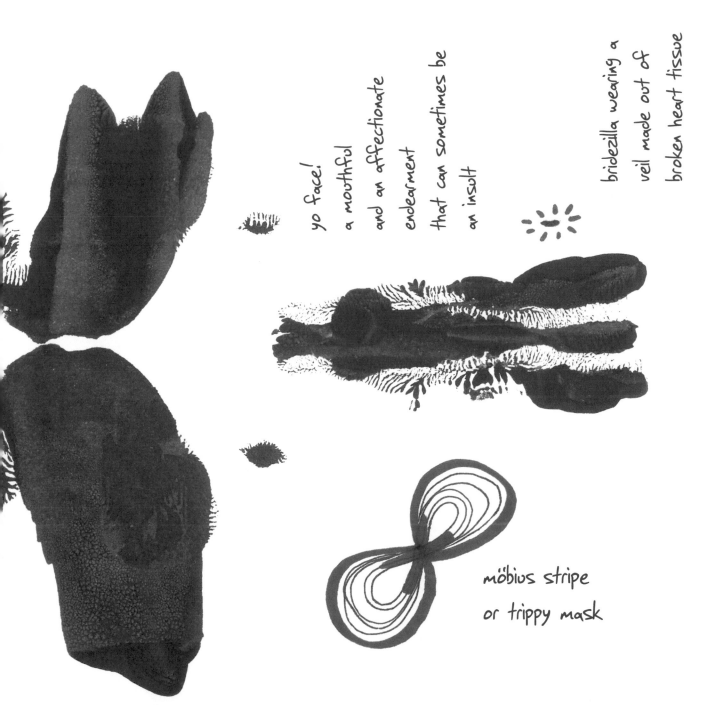

yo face!
a mouthful
and an affectionate
endearment
that can sometimes be
an insult

bridezilla wearing a
veil made out of
broken heart tissue

möbius stripe
or trippy mask

to create is the best path
to knowing who you are
and to designing who you
become

body mask also known as a
dress

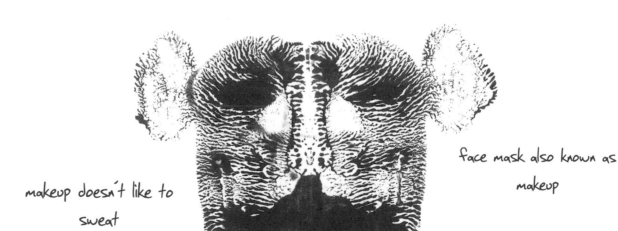

makeup doesn't like to
sweat

face mask also known as
makeup

just fucking admit you couldn't come up with a name

untitled

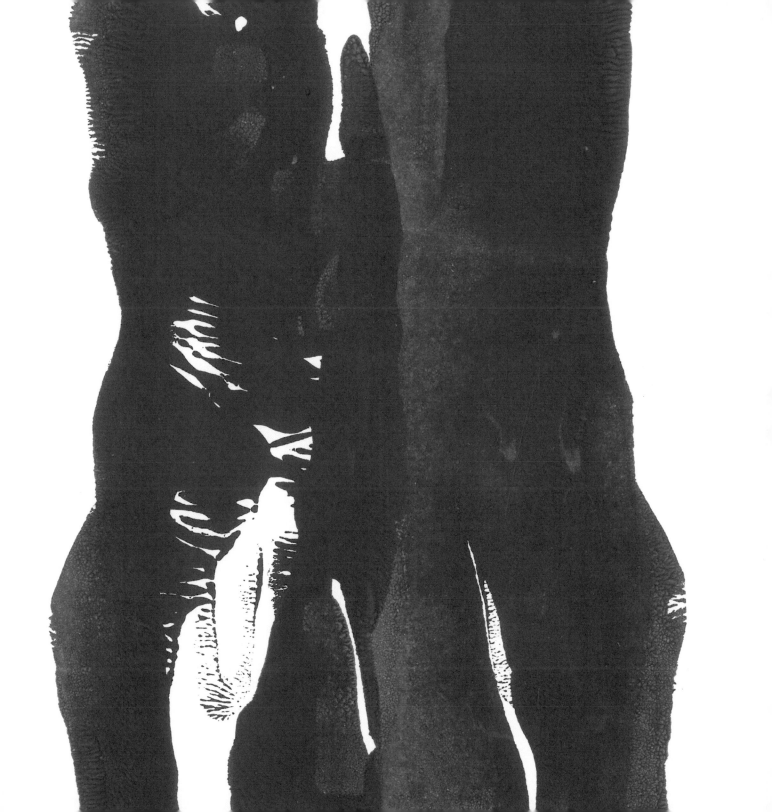

there's a thing inside you
that isn't you
or not the you you know
or could easily describe
it sees you better than
you see yourself
and if you give it half a chance
it may yet teach you something

the subconscious

gene-rosity starts off with a gene
and it's not just any gene
it's that elusive one that doesn't
make it into biology class
though it may be the cornerstone
of all that lives
what is not shared will not last

with feet up in the air

even a happy child knows it's not all fun and bubble gum

the difference between
perfectionism
and the pursuit of excellence
is like the difference between
transactional sex and an open-ended collaboration

chasing the next point
or two titans carrying hand grenades

Dear reader,

This is for you. Has anybody told you they love you today, and that you matter oh so very much? Well I do, and you do. You see, without you, I wouldn't be doing what I love, so thank you— from the big fat buttocks of my heart thank you!

And this is also for me. I never got to discover my inner child until I was a grown-up, and after I decided to meet this magical being, I found out that I couldn't get enough of Her/Him/It. I also got to know that she is much smarter, wiser, and funnier than I had been led to believe— in short the best fucking BFF and teacher I could ever hope for. I'm not sure what I did to deserve her, but blessings are not about what we deserve, are they?

I hope to meet your inner child someday.

Mine and yours forever,

koshi

PS: oh and you've got to come to Accra— the sexiest coconut trees alive and roasted plantains!

a meeting of both hearts and minds

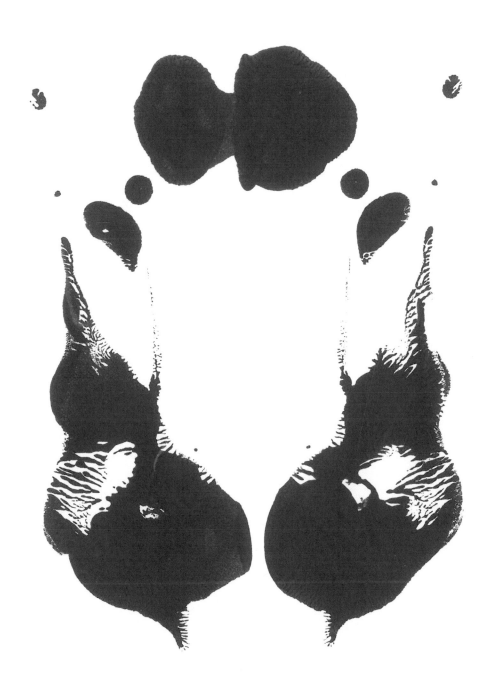

Archway Publishing books may be ordered through booksellers or by contacting:

Archway Publishing
1663 Liberty Drive
Bloomington, IN 47403
www.archwaypublishing.com
844-669-3957

ISBN: 978-1-6657-2089-2 (sc)
ISBN: 978-1-6657-2090-8 (hc)
ISBN: 978-1-6657-2091-5 (e)

Library of Congress Control Number: 2022905487

Print information available on the last page.

Archway Publishing rev. date: 09/27/2022

Printed in the United States
by Baker & Taylor Publisher Services